Piglets

Belong to

Pigs

SCHOLASTIC

Children's Press®
A Division of Scholastic Inc.
New York Toronto London Auckland Sydney Mexico City
New Delhi Hong Kong Danbury, Connecticut

Early Childhood Consultants:

Ellen Booth Church
Diane Ohanesian

1 2 3 4 5 6 7 8 9 10 R 19 18 17 16 15 14 13 12 11 10   62

Library of Congress Cataloging-in-Publication Data

Piglets belong to pigs.
    p. cm. — (Rookie preschool)
ISBN-13: 978-0-531-24408-1 (lib. bdg.)   ISBN-13: 978-0-531-24583-5 (pbk.)
ISBN-10: 0-531-24408-3 (lib. bdg.)   ISBN-10: 0-531-24583-7 (pbk.)
    Includes bibliographical references and index.
    1. Domestic animals—Infancy—Juvenile literature. 2. Domestic animals—Juvenile literature. I. Title.
SF75.5.P54 2009
636'.07 – dc22   2009012174

A **duckling**

wing

beak

belongs to a **duck**.

A kitten

paw

belongs to a
cat.

tail

A kid belongs

hoof

horn

to a **goat.**

What do you think of **that?**

A **calf** belongs

hoof

to a **COW.**

A **foal** belongs

hoof

to a **horse.**

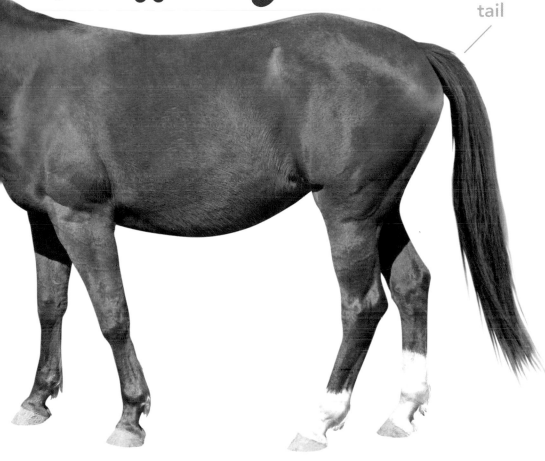

tail

11

A **lamb** belongs

—— hoof

to a **Sheep**. Mommies love babies, of course!

A **puppy** belongs

paw —

to a **dog.**

A chick belongs

beak

to a **hen.**

tail

wing

A **piglet**

belongs
to a
pig.

hoof

tail

Let's say it all again!

 A **piglet**

 belongs to a **pig.**

And everyone belongs on a
farm!

Words to Know

Can you name the animals you saw in this book?

Cat   Kitten

Goat   Kid

Duckling   Duck

Calf   Cow

22

Chick   Chicken

Puppy   Dog

Lamb   Sheep

Foal   Horse

Rookie Storytime Tips

. . . .

Piglets Belong to Pigs is a gentle introduction to the names of animal babies. As you and your preschooler read this book together, guide him or her in pointing to and naming the different parts of the animals' bodies. It's a great way to build vocabulary!

. . . .

Invite your child to find the following. As you both go back through the book, your child will reinforce his or her recognition of animals and animal babies, a key preschool skill.

Can you find this mommy's baby? What is it called?

Can you find this baby's mommy? What is she called?

Can you find this baby's mommy? What kind of animal is she?

Can you find this mommy's baby? What is it called?

What sound does a sheep make?
What sound does a duck make?
What sound does a horse make?